Jay Rayner is an award-winning writer, journalist and broadcaster with a fine collection of floral shirts. He has written on everything from crime and politics, through cinema and theatre, to the visual arts, but is best known as restaurant critic for the *Observer*. For a while he was a sex columnist for *Cosmopolitan*; he also once got himself completely waxed in the name of journalism. He only mentions this because it hurt. Jay is a former Young Journalist of the Year, Critic of the Year and Restaurant Critic of the Year, though not all in the same year. Somehow he has also found time to write four novels and three works of non-fiction. He presents *The Kitchen Cabinet* for BBC Radio 4 and is a regular on British television, where he is familiar as a judge on *MasterChef* and, since 2009, as the resident food expert on *The One Show*. He likes pig.

My Dining Hell

Twenty Ways to Have a Lousy Night Out

JAY RAYNER

PENGUIN BOOKS

PENGUIN BOOKS

UK | USA | Canada | Ireland | Australia
India | New Zealand | South Africa

Penguin Books is part of the Penguin Random House group of companies
whose addresses can be found at global.penguinrandomhouse.com.

First published in the *Observer* and the *London Magazine*
1999, 2000, 2003, 2005, 2007, 2008, 2009, 2010, 2011, 2012
Published as a Penguin ebook 2012
Published in Penguin Books 2015
005

Copyright © Jay Rayner Limited, 2012, 2015

The moral right of the author has been asserted

Set in 11/13 pt Dante MT Std
Typeset by Jouve (UK), Milton Keynes
Printed in Great Britain by Clays Ltd, St Ives plc

A CIP catalogue record for this book is available from the British Library
ISBN : 978-0-241-97347-9

www.greenpenguin.co.uk

MIX
Paper from
responsible sources
FSC® C018179

Penguin Random House is committed to a
sustainable future for our business, our readers
and our planet. This book is made from Forest
Stewardship Council® certified paper.

Contents

Contents

Acknowledgements

All but two of the restaurant reviews collected here – those of Le Caprice and Salloos – first appeared in the *Observer* newspaper. I am grateful to Guardian Newspapers Limited for granting me the rights to republish them as part of this collection. I would also like to thank Roger Alton, and his successor as editor of the *Observer*, John Mulholland, for allowing me to live the dream as the paper's restaurant critic. Likewise, I am indebted to the various editors of the *Observer Magazine*, where my reviews have appeared since 1999 and who are, in chronological order, Sheryl Garratt, Allan Jenkins and Ruaridh Nicoll. The reviews of Le Caprice and Salloos originally appeared in the *London Magazine*. I would like to thank my editors there, first Laura Tennant and now Lucinda Bredin.

This book is dedicated to the myriad dining companions who shared these meals with me. They ate the food so you wouldn't have to.

Introduction

You are a horrible person. Oh sure, you like to think otherwise. You think of yourself as kind and giving. You remember your friends' birthdays, feed their pets when they are away, talk in a sweet, non-patronizing manner to their children. And yet, when presented with the chance to buy a book filled with accounts of twenty restaurants – their chefs, their owners, their poor benighted front-of-house staff – getting a complete stiffing courtesy of the sort of vitriolic blood-curdling review that would make their loved ones seethe and the victims call for their mummies, you seized it with both hands.

Or perhaps you didn't. Perhaps this book was given to you. Oh dear. If that's the case then the situation is far worse. That means it's the friend or relation who gave it to you who thinks you are a horrible person; the sort who would get a real kick out of this volume.

Don't worry. You are not alone. I have been a restaurant critic for over a decade, written reviews of well over 700 establishments, and if there is one thing I have learned in that time, it is that people like reviews of bad restaurants. No, scratch that. They adore them, feast upon them like starving vultures who have spotted fly-blown carrion out in the bush for the first time in weeks. They like to claim otherwise, of course. Readers of restaurant reviews like to present themselves as private arbiters of taste; as people interested in the good stuff. I'm sure they are. I'm sure they really do care whether the steak was served *au point* as requested, whether the jus showed that joyful accident of technique and good taste, whether the soufflé had achieved a certain ineffable lightness.

And yet, when I compare dinner to bodily fluids, the room to an S&M chamber in Neasden (only without the glamour or class) and the bill to an act of grand larceny, why, then the baying crowd is truly happy. Certainly I know that had I, in a moment of gross self-importance, decided to compile a selection of all my reviews, the good, the bad and the indifferent, I would have grown tired quickly of being told by people that while they loved the book with all their hearts, the pieces they had really enjoyed, the ones that really did it for them, were the complete stinkers.

This is not surprising. The fact is that bad experiences make for better narratives than good ones. As Leo Tolstoy once famously said – and it's always worth pressing into service one of the Russian greats in defence of a book dripping with bile – 'Happy families are all alike; every unhappy family is unhappy in its own way.' Exactly the same applies to restaurants. Eat in a good one and its virtues are so simple, so obvious, so shared: there are tables with chairs around them; there are nice, personable people to bring food to you from the kitchen, and the decor of the room in which you sit is comfortable without being overtly showy or distracting. Then there is the food itself, which is classy and makes complete sense. None of the ingredients have been tortured. Eating in these restaurants is a huge pleasure; writing about them, however, a little less so. The language of the overwhelmingly positive can be a strain. Before you know it you are lurching into accounts of angels' kisses; of the delicate flapping of butterfly wings against your downed cheek; of silken bed linen and sun-dappled glades and dewy-eyed kittens. The meals can be satisfying, the writing about them a quick route to acute nausea.

Ah, but bad restaurant reviews. Now that is a different matter entirely. There is, it seems, absolutely no end to the human ability to fuck things up: to have really stupid ideas and then throw wheelbarrow-loads of cash at making them a reality. And now the vocabulary to describe it all opens up before you. We are in the landscape of atrocity, and there is almost no comparison that cannot be pressed into service. Suddenly dinner becomes a slaughterhouse or a battlefield, a set of socially communicable diseases or a car crash in slow motion on the M6, complete with the emergency services and rubbernecking. It is easy to prove that most people read positive restaurant reviews for vicarious pleasure; if I write a good review the restaurant may, praise be, receive a few bookings or even, by their standards, a large number of bookings, but it will still be a relatively tiny number compared to those who actually read the review. In short my power and influence is negligible, beyond providing a distraction for about ten minutes. Readers may get some enjoyment at second hand from reading about the lovely time I had – witness my charmed life – but it rarely goes much beyond that.

By the same token, people read bad reviews for

vicarious *dis*pleasure. Every time I disembowel a place, they feel I am taking revenge on that particular restaurant for all the truly shitty meals they themselves have ever had anywhere. In the age of Web 2.0, when any article comes complete with online reader comments, it can feel like a virtual mob has gathered about the victim to shout: 'Kill them! Kill them a lot!'

It would be tempting therefore to fill every column with vitriol, to spray blood and guts across every page, electronic or otherwise. It's a temptation I try to resist. In the closing moments of the animated modern classic *Ratatouille* – which, incidentally, is pretty much the only movie about restaurant kitchens that chefs will agree captures accurately the mood and culture of such places – the restaurant critic Anton Ego delivers a gloriously well-observed speech which had all of us who do this job hanging our heads in shame. 'In many ways,' he intoned, in the cognac-soaked voice of Peter O''Toole, 'the work of a critic is easy. We risk very little yet enjoy a position over those who offer up their work and their selves to our judgement. We thrive on negative criticism, which is fun to write and to read. But the bitter truth we critics must face is that, in the grand scheme of things, the average piece of junk is probably more meaningful than our criticism designating it so.' Amen.

That doesn't mean the negative review is a bad thing. If a restaurant is charging north of £60 a head for dinner and serves up an experience you will only recover from courtesy of a good Jungian therapist, a pitcher of vodka and a prescription of Prozac, they deserve to be called on it. Likewise, a 'how not to' manual can be as helpful as a 'how to' manual. If you are thinking of opening a restaurant (don't) and manage to steer clear of all the mind-numbingly stupid mistakes encountered in the restaurants reviewed here, you just might be on to something. See how kind I am? I am offering cruel laughs and education all at the same time.

Still, the bad review does have to be handled carefully. I would be lying if I claimed I never went to a restaurant knowing it was going to be awful. And yet with places like Shumi, Divo or Abracadabra, it was irresistible. My job is less to review restaurants than to find something to write about, in as entertaining a manner as possible, and some writing opportunities cannot be passed up. Hell, the urinals at Abracadabra are in the shape of women's red-lipsticked mouths. Who wouldn't want to write about that? Don't believe me? Go and have a read. I can wait.

Done? See what I mean? Good.

Nevertheless, most of the time I go to restaurants carrying a ballast of hope. I am greedy. I always want to eat well. So shoot me. And frankly, given how often I have terrible experiences while looking for the good stuff, I really don't need to hunt down the bad, for it is always out there, and often obscuring the good. It is one of the more frustrating features of British restaurants that a great kitchen can be let down by staggeringly stupid decor or can knock out some dishes that are terrific and yet others that make you want to punch someone. Some awful restaurants don't even have it in them to be uniformly awful. In some of these reviews I occasionally have to say nice things. It can't be helped.

But what of the impact of the reviews I write? While I have received a few legal letters over the years, from restaurateurs taking a punt that they just might be able to get me to retract what I have said, none of them have been successful. I know the laws of libel. I know the difference between fair comment ('The soup tasted like it came from a packet, which is remarkable given they must have made it themselves') and a blatant untruth ('The soup came from a packet'). I occasionally receive letters or emails from friends and relations of the chefs – usually it's the chef's mother – asking me if I have any idea how it feels to have your life's work slagged off in a review. And I quickly reply: yes, I know exactly how it feels. I have published a number of other books, both novels and non-fiction, and while, happily, I have received good reviews, I have also had ten tons of crap kicked out of me, both in newspapers and online.

Yes, it hurts, but I never question the right of anybody to express an opinion. There are much worse jobs than writing for a living, just as there much worse jobs than cooking for a living. If we're charging good money for a product that is, essentially, an expression of our ego, the customer has the right to say what they think of it if they find fault. Just to prove it, and to balance things out a little, you will find no 'Praise for the author' in this book. Instead there's an 'Abuse for the author' section, full of disobliging things people have said about me, both online and off.

Subsequent to the publication of many of the reviews collected here, the restaurants closed. Was it my review or, for that matter, the equally acerbic review of one of my so-called rivals that did for it? I genuinely don't think so. We might be able to help good restaurants along, but bad restaurants fail all by themselves. We are the doctors who diagnose the disease, the pallbearers who carry out the coffin. We are not the assassins with the razor-sharp stiletto in the toe of our shoe. And while it's always sad when a business folds, if it takes out a truly awful restaurant, that has to be better for the industry than not.

Not that it means there are fewer bad restaurants. As each one closes, another opens. Lessons are never learned, stupidity never vanquished. Rip-offs, like bad steaks, are always with us. Indeed the bad review is really nothing new. As long as there have been meals there have been rude things written and said about them. For example, as a young man, Winston Churchill was asked about a dinner he had attended the night before. 'Well,' he replied, 'it would have been splendid . . . if the wine had been as cold as the soup, the beef as rare as the service, the brandy as old as the fish, and the maid as willing as the duchess.'

God, but I wish I'd written that.

Abuse for the author

From a review of Jay Rayner's non-fiction book *The Man Who Ate the World* (2008), by Nicholas Blincoe, published in the *Daily Telegraph*, April 2008:

'If *The Man Who Ate the World* was dinner, it would be the dog's . . . [It] might be a mess but, in its dream-like logic, it succeeds in laying bare the desires and fears that motivate its author. Rayner is the restaurant critic of the *Observer*, yet as he lumbers from one eye-wateringly expensive gaff to another, a suspicion takes root. Is it possible that Rayner not only does not know what he is doing, but that he is in a state of abject panic? The feeling grows as the pages slip away: is his book an elaborate cry for help? Then, just before the end, Rayner says it out loud: perhaps he "wasn't a connoisseur at all, just a greedy man with an expense account".'

For Jay Rayner's novel *The Oyster House Siege* (2007), from Amazon.co.uk:

'If this book was a meal in a restaurant it would be returned to the chef as indigestible. The plot is poorly thought out, the characterization is amateurish and the book is so badly written that many paragraphs have to be read three times before a reader can grasp what the writer meant. Any time spent reading this book is a waste.'

From Twitter, 2010:

'Jay Rayner is a good writer but has a face for radio, bless him.'

'Jay Rayner . . . food critic, TV presenter. A face like monkfish genitalia and so ugly it makes you gasp.'

From a review of Jay Rayner's novel *Day of Atonement* (1998), posted on Amazon:

'The cover of the book, simulating a can of Campbell's chicken soup, gives one a clear indication of its nature – tinny, thin in substance, and containing lots of nasty things which you wish never to discover. Although the book is described as comic, my advice is to enjoy the cover, as this is the only mildly amusing thing which it has to offer.'

The legal small print

All restaurant reviews are a snapshot of a moment in time, and should be understood as such. The date at the top of the review indicates when it was published. Any notes about what may or may not have happened to the restaurant since publication are included at the end of the relevant review. The vast majority of the restaurants reviewed here have now ceased trading in the form under which they were reviewed.

A victory of style over content: Or . . . what the hell were they thinking?

November 2003

Shumi, 23 St James's Street, London SW1. Telephone: 020 7747 9380. Price of dinner for two, anything would be too much.

A short while after arriving at Shumi – after having been ignored by two sets of receptionists, one on the ground floor and one on the first, after having been seated at a table beneath which were scattered shards of broken glass and being moved to another – I was approached by a thin, suited man with an orange perma-tan. He was tall, had the posture of a praying mantis, and wore shimmering blue reflective wrap-around shades, which he did not have the good grace to remove before talking to me. He leaned down and said: 'Welcome to Shumi. I hope your experience is . . .' Then he stood up and walked away.

I was baffled. You hope my experience is . . . what exactly? Over soon? Not too psychologically damaging? Or maybe it was just a moment of Cartesian philosophizing on the part of a restaurateur who now recognized he had opened one of the most irritating restaurants in London dining history. He simply wanted my time there to 'be'; for it not to engender any response at all. To which I can only say: no chance, mate.

Ah Shumi, how do I hate thee? Let me count the ways. I hate the meeters and greeters who run around trying not to catch your eye. I hate the battered old escalators which look like hand-me-downs from the Elephant and Castle shopping centre. I hate the nasty, white-out decor of grubby tiles and three-quarter-length net curtains and I hate the asphyxiating prices. But most of all I hate the concept. Shumi is a Japanese restaurant serving Italian food. Or an Italian restaurant where the food is served Japanese-style. So you get to eat risotto with chopsticks. Hurrah! That's an idea we've been waiting for, isn't it? There's also a 'paccio bar', where 'Italian sushi' is prepared, by which they mean carpaccios of meat or fish. I don't usually quote press releases but this one deserves its moment in the sun. 'The tastes that you will experience will be typically Italian, but you may find that we have taken an Eastern Road to get there.' Now I get it. You thought this up during a booze-fuelled bender down the A13 to Southend.

The only way Shumi might have worked is if the food were truly exceptional, but it isn't. The best I can say is, it isn't offensive. Fragile slices of beef dressed with olive oil were fine. A 'mosaic' of raw monkfish and tuna was less interesting than the shreds of confited aubergine that came with it. Saffron squid tasted neither of fish nor saffron. A main course of roast John Dory was completely over-salted. Agro-dolce – or bitter-sweet – duck was pleasant and nutty but not £18-a-shot pleasant. And £5 for the Shumi Espresso plate – lukewarm coffee, a chocolate, a shot glass of vodka-drenched sorbet – was not 'pretty special', as the waitress had claimed. It was a collection of disparate objects arranged on a tray as if for a memory test at a children's party.

Our waitress, it must be said, was sweetness itself and should be able to find less socially divisive employment, perhaps by turning to a life of crime. We asked her what 'Shumi' meant. She said it might be Japanese for 'Hush', which is the name of the owners' other London restaurant (one of whom is Roger Moore's son Geoffrey, he of the orange tan). Then again, she said, it might also be the name of a Bond Girl, which got us thinking. If you're going to name restaurants after Bond girls why not open one called Pussy Galore? That would surely drag in the punters, as long as it was not a false promise.

Our bill, without a single drop of overpriced alcohol, would have been nudging the ton were it not for the opening week 25 per cent food discount and I gave thanks that it was not my money. Even with that saving grace I was left with this one thought: Shumi was two hours of my life that I'll never get back.

Shumi closed in 2004. Asked by an industry magazine about the restaurant, its co-founder Jamie Barber said: 'Some people say Shumi wasn't a successful restaurant, but I disagree. I say it was an unmitigated disaster. I think we got everything right except for the design, the service, the menu, the pricing and the execution. It was an extremely difficult period.' Barber has gone on to launch a number of successful restaurant brands. They are better than Shumi. Which isn't difficult.

April 2008

Abracadabra, 91 Jermyn Street, London SW1. Telephone: 020 7930 3222. But only if you're feeling brave. Meal for two, including wine and service, £100.

Abracadabra isn't so much a restaurant as a random sequence of events. I could describe it as bad – and believe me, the food is, in a very special way – but that really doesn't do the experience justice. It sits on London's Jermyn Street, alongside all the posh shirt-makers and places selling expensive shiny stuff you don't need but want anyway. And then there's the entrance to Abracadabra, a tarnished Top Shop brooch on an Armani jacket. It's marked by a dour man in a jester's suit looking like he's waiting either for death or to be arrested, if only as an escape from the loneliness.

Down the stairs, walled in a harlequin print, and we're in a fancy restaurant, though one as imagined by a thirteen-year-old girl who's been at her mum's sherry. The floor is a multi-coloured mosaic. There's a giant Father Christmas made from chocolate. The lamps have female legs in stockings. There is risqué art of the sort that would get the thirteen-year-old girl's slightly older brother horny. The chairs are all golden spray-painted thrones. There are piles of Russian-language newspapers. Apparently one of the tables flips over to reveal bondage equipment. If only I was dressed for it.

Abracadabra was opened two years ago by Dave West, who made his millions in cash-and-carry booze at Calais.

Big bloke. Pink suit. Three chins. Hates the smoking ban. Hates it so much that the first question we're asked is: 'Smoking or non-smoking?' Hang on. Isn't that illegal? But we don't argue, and say: 'Non-smoking, please.' So we're shown to a love booth, my mate Mark and I. Fixed into the ceiling above the table is a TV screen showing Sky news on a loop. Lots of stuff about the Mills–McCartney divorce.

To our left we see something more terrifying. Dave West is so against the smoking ban he hired Cherie Blair to challenge her own husband's law, and here's a huge picture of her cheek to cheek with Dave. Mark is a film editor and knows how to look into people's eyes. 'She's saying: "Help me, please. Somebody."' She stares at us throughout dinner, balefully. A leaflet on the table declares that Abracadabra has the most extensive wine list in London. It isn't the most extensive but it is the weirdest. It runs from a Methuselah of Cristal champagne for £29,000 to Blue Nun at £20. In between is their own label. It's called the Dog's Bollocks. Well, of course it is.

We decide to eat something, more as a macho challenge than out of hunger. It's pizzas and pasta with a few fancy things of the sort that get made on *Ready Steady Cook* just as the time is running out. My shallot tarte tatin is full of slippery undercooked grey onions with undercooked pastry topped by a disc of completely uncooked goat's cheese. It glues my tongue to the roof of my mouth. Mark gets a crayfish cocktail with a Marie Rose sauce which, remarkably, is an exact match for that pink gloopy stuff from a bottle.

For my main I have the Kobe burger. Kobe is the most expensive breed of cattle in the world. According to the menu this Kobe is raised on a diet of 'race-horse grass', beer and massages. There are blokes down my local pub who would kill for a life like that. Kobe is prized because of its marbling and its texture. So what's the point of putting it through a bloody mincer? The burger is dry and black. It costs £18. I mourn the cow. To give credit, Mark's duck breast is fine, but everything else has been tortured in the kitchen. 'The pak choi is overcooked to a point my mother might approve of,' Mark says. He's a Yorkshireman.

I nip to the toilet, seeking entertainment. I get it. The urinals are big, red-lipsticked women's mouths because obviously there's nothing a chap likes more than to wee into one of those. In the cubicle the toilet is rested on a sculpture of a naked woman so you sit on her lap to evacuate. Hurrah. Apparently in the ladies, all the taps are golden penises, modelled on Dave West's own engorged member. I wonder if anybody drinks straight from them?

Back at the table I'm told there is no lemon tart. I suggest punishing the chef. 'He's actually a good guy,' says the charming waiter, 'but sometimes he needs shooting.' You don't say? Cherie watches me eat a mediocre chocolate fondant, we pay the bill and, gratefully, climb the stairs back up to the real world.

In the early hours of 12 December 2014, Dave West was found stabbed to death in the street outside his home, behind the restaurant. His son, also called David, was later charged with his killing.

November 2008

Buddha Bar, 8 Victoria Embankment, London WC2. Telephone: 020 3371 7777 (but please don't). Meal for two, including wine and service, £175.

One of the curiosities of this week's restaurant – along with 'How do they live with themselves?' and 'Why isn't there a baying mob outside with pitchforks and burning torches?' – is that it should be named after a deity whose followers are famed for their serenity and yet should be capable of engendering in me such a blind, raging spittle-flecked fury. There will be casualties in the restaurant trade as a result of the current economic turmoil; I sincerely hope London's Buddha Bar is one of them.

I should have given up after the hassle of booking. Not merely the five minutes of thrashing hold music nor the irritating demand for my first name (and my usual reply that I only wanted to book a table, not be their pen friend), but also the requirement that I supply an email address. Why? 'Because it's the only way we can confirm you have a reservation.' Really? So putting the name down in a book, the method that's worked for a century or more, isn't good enough? Absolutely not, for when the email arrives it reveals that any table booked before 10 p.m. must be given back within two hours and that, while there is a bar, they don't guarantee you'll be allowed into it. There is a particular word I could use here, but I refuse to denigrate the honest pleasures of self-abuse purely to make a point.

The London Buddha Bar is part of an international chain. Previously I visited the outpost in Dubai and was struck there by the late-middle age of the male clientele, and the oestrogen-rich youth of their friends who were doubtless their nieces. Here, as there, hedge-fund-sized buckets of cash have been spent on filling an empty space (under Waterloo Bridge) with gargantuan Asian artefacts and then turning the lights down so low you can't see any of them. The only one you can see is the enormous Buddha; even as a diehard, to-the-barricades atheist I find the exploitation of a religious symbol like this offensive. There is just enough light by which to read the pan-Asian menu, which was a shame, because it meant we could order.

The food is that killer combination of stupendously clumsy and grossly overpriced. Ten pounds' worth of wok-fried salt-and-pepper calamari and frog's legs was leathery, greasy and unrelenting. The only contrast came from the frog's legs, which promised a little light haemorrhage as the hidden bones punctured your mouth. Worse, and £5 more expensive, was the crayfish and crawfish summer roll, speaking gloomily of an Icelandic summer of wind and rain and general hardship: flavourless crayfish, mushy avocado, dull shredded carrots. The rice-based wrap was so dry and thick as to be edible, but only if you had no choice. We did, so we didn't.

Next, some sushi: £3 a piece, minimum order two pieces. I looked at the unglossy lozenge of tuna. I ran my finger along its edge. It was dry and hard, as if it had been cut long before being plated. Eel and turbot were lifeless. Of the main courses the most cynical was £26 for a meagre portion of Korean seared beef, tender but taste-less in and of itself, then smeared with a pungent – read unpleasant – tomato sauce. In an attempt to complete the tour of Asia we also had a Thai-style red curry with shrimp, and it was indeed in the style of a Thai curry much as Zimbabwe is in the style of a democracy. The small shrimps – seven of them for £16.50 – were served mixed in with rice inside the husk of a coconut, with the slick of red curry sauce in a saucer on the side. I genu-inely do not understand how any self-respecting kitchen can serve up trash like this, at these prices, and still find the will to get up in the morning.

And so to dessert: 'The best part of the meal,' as the waiter said. 'We live in hope,' I replied. Only to have it dashed, for the Buddha Bar is where hope, like the ingre-dients, goes to die. A chocolate fondue for £12.50 – sorry to go on about the prices, but really – brought something congealing in a bowl, without a burner to keep it mov-ing, some friable, dusty meringues, a couple of crumbly biscuits of the sort that are served after Jewish funerals, and a little flavour-free fruit. Was there anything to rec-ommend the place? Yes, our waiter, who was cheerful and friendly and efficient and completely wasted here. Save yourself, my friend. Get a job elsewhere. You don't deserve this. And frankly, neither did we.

This branch of Buddha Bar closed in May 2010, a welcome vic-tim of the recession. However, a new Buddha Bar opened in Knightsbridge in November 2012.

March 2005

Cocoon, 65 Regent Street, London W1. Telephone: 020 7494 7600. Meal for two, including wine and service, £110.

Cocoon feels like it was specifically designed with me in my mind. Specifically designed so I would hate it. Let's create the kind of place Rayner would loathe, they might have said to each other. There has to be a market for that. And so it has proved. On the night we went, this long, curving room on a first floor overlooking London's Regent Street was heaving with lipstick-slicked women wearing berets at a jaunty angle and men in mid-thigh jackets. Some of the men even had ponytails. How I regretted leaving the cattle prod at home.

At Cocoon hate springs eternal. I hated the thumping music. I hated the wispy flounces of net hanging floor to ceiling, which, like shower curtains, reached out to grab you. I hated the ceiling centrepieces of red ruched fabric pushed into a central hole, which decorated every one of the separate spaces and looked like cat's arses. I hated the clipboard Nazi at the front door, and the bar area with its crumb-crusted seats from the previous occupants and the floor walkers with their earpieces who still managed to run around like headless chickens when we tried to get shown to our table.

And then there was the menu. Like so many places in London this year it is pan-Asian (I could throw away the knife and fork for the rest of the year if I fancied). It therefore says things like: 'The tastes we prepare have no prescribed order' and 'We are here to guide you towards following your own path', a couple of quotes from the *Bumper Book of Over-conceptualized Restaurant Bollocks*. The document itself, which is cluttered and fiendishly difficult to read in the moody half-light, includes sections covering Japan, China and Thailand. I like eating the food of all those places, but not necessarily at the same time and certainly not when it's done with so little accomplishment. Why eat bad Thai food here when you can eat it so much better just across the street? Why eat lousy Japanese here when you can get the real thing round the corner?

Even the good stuff didn't make an argument for the place. A basket of very fresh steamed mixed dim sum at an ambitious £12.50 showed there is someone in the kitchen who knows what they are doing. Scallop shumai and Chinese chive dumplings, in particular, had a real clarity of flavour to them. But why eat them here when you could go to Royal China or Harbour City or Yauatcha or Hakkasan for a wider selection? We also liked a hybrid salad of seared beef, with very tender meat and a good selection of leaves, but £10 seemed to be pushing it.

The rest was lacklustre. Nigiri sushi, around £6 for two pieces, was very average. Salt-and-pepper pork had a soggy batter, which suggested it had hung about in the kitchen before being delivered. Pad Thai, £7.50 worth of it, was watery and bland. Baby spinach steamed with garlic was under-seasoned. And a Japanese-style foie gras roll with a slick of sour but otherwise flavourless plum compote was one of the nastiest things I have eaten in a very long time. The pâté needs to be partnered with crunch – brioche, toast – not the mush of rice.

All of this is irrelevant, of course, because nobody who comes to Cocoon comes for the food. They come for the scene and to be seen. They come to hang their nimble legs off the bar stools and to sip drinks called Martinis which aren't, in such number that, by the time they get to the table, you could serve them one of Charlie Chaplin's old boots decorated with a chive flower and they would be happy. Slap them with a bill for over a ton and they would still hug themselves with pleasure. Cocoon? Personally, I think they should have stopped at the first syllable of the name. They would have had it about right.

Cocoon closed in 2011, after a successful six years in business. After a number of incarnations the site is now occupied by the highly regarded steak and seafood restaurant Hawksmoor Air Street.

2

Because I can get away with saying it

July 2007

Bloom's, 130 Golders Green Road, London NW11. Telephone: 020 8455 1338. Meal for two, including service, £60.

I once said that bad restaurants were like car crashes and chest infections, in that they were never sought but were, instead, something that just happened to me. After my dinner at the Jewish restaurant Bloom's, in Golders Green, north-west London, I realized the analogy goes further. You also feel the effects for days afterwards. Every time I let slip an involuntary belch, which was often, I was right back there at the table, and that was not a good place to be. Never has the late journalist John Diamond's great joke about Jewish keep-fit lessons – eat three bowls of lockshen pudding, press your hand to your chest and say: 'Feel the burn' – been so true.

My wife, the shicksa, says I have no one to blame for this but myself. She believes the entire repertoire of Eastern Europe's Ashkenazi Jews is very bad food, and that my affection for it comes from a blindness brought about by entrenched cultural associations. I think she is both wrong and right. I would never argue that this culinary tradition, which makes a virtue of chicken fat, the deep-fat fryer and the boiling of perfectly good pieces of meat, is refined. But I would also say that there is both good bad food and bad bad food. The food I was served at Bloom's was, for the most part, very bad bad food indeed.

It should not have been this way. Bloom's is an institution. Mind you, so is the high-security psychiatric hospital at Broadmoor, and nobody would ever go there for dinner. Still, it has lineage, stretching back decades. There used to be two of them, but the Whitechapel branch closed a decade ago, partly because it mislaid its kosher licence. Recently I learned that the interior of the Golders Green outpost had been given a makeover, and indeed it has. It is all sleek booths and shiny glass panels. Out has gone the mural of Jerusalem street life. In comes something in rainbow shades depicting the wandering of the Jews through the desert. It has odd touches, not least that Moses appears to be holding the Ten Commandments at the mouth of the divided Red Sea, as the children of Israel trail away into the distance leaving him behind. Perhaps they had worked out where he was taking them for dinner and were trying to escape.

Let me tell you what's good. The new green pickles were good. They were crunchy and garlicky as they should be. The coarse and earthy chopped liver with which I started would also have been good had it not travelled so swiftly from fridge to the table. As for everything else, it might have been better if it had stayed in the fridge and not troubled the table at all. My companion, a food blogger called Silverbrow (google 'Silverbrow on food'), who takes the blame for my eating here, ordered the fried gefilte fish. This mixture of sweetened and minced white fish should be crisp on the outside and light and fluffy on the inside. This one was flat, the size of a dinner plate and denser than Jade Goody. I imagined it having its own gravitational field, and dragging planets out of alignment. I tried a little with some crane, a mixture of beetroot and horseradish, and was immediately reminded of my paternal grandmother. This was not a good thing. I didn't like my father's mother.

For my main I ordered salt beef, which, done right, is a thing of beauty. This was done wrong. It was extraordinarily dry for something that spends the entire cooking process in liquid. I had also asked that it not be too lean. A little fat is what makes the dish; it adds a rich slipperiness to the soft meat. Instead, they brought it out with a lump of fat on the side, and I was supposed to combine the two myself. This isn't how it works. The fat should be attached and then you pretend you are simply eating your way through dinner, rather than actively making yourself a candidate for angioplasty. The latke it came with was merely the hot, salty cousin of the gefilte fish.

Silverbrow's gedempte meatballs, served in a gloopy cornflour-thickened sauce the same shade of orange as Dale Winton, were, if anything, worse. 'Gedempte' usually means 'long cooked', so that they fall apart. Here 'gedempte' took on an onomatopoeic quality, as of the sound a boulder makes when dropped into water. They were solid, as though the meat had been blitzed to a paste before cooking. None of this was cheap. Think £18.90 for the salt beef and £12.50 for the meatballs.

We pushed on to dessert because we are Jews and this is what we do. Both the apple strudel and lockshen pudding, a curious confection of sweetened noodles with sultanas, had a flaccid texture and violent heat, as if warmed through in the special fast oven. They came with custard, which was watery and, unlike these two diners, thin. The menu optimistically invites its clientele to 'taste the quality'. The best I think you can hope for is to feel the width.

This, the last remaining branch of Bloom's, closed in June 2010 after forty-five years in business. On the one hand this is a great loss. On the other hand, having eaten the food, not so much. The gag about Jade Goody's density underlines the way journalism can only capture a particular moment in time. At the point it was written Ms Goody was still representative of a special sort of crass celebrity culture which makes stars of people who have no good reason to be paid any attention. She was yet to be sanctified on account of her diagnosis with, and eventual death from, cancer.

November 2007

Divo, 12 Waterloo Place, London SW1. Telephone: 020 7484 1355. Meal for two, including wine and service, £140.

A little over a century ago my Jewish forebears fled that part of Eastern Europe then known as the Pale of Settlement. Having eaten at Divo, described as London's first luxury Ukrainian restaurant, I now know why. It was to escape the cooking. There are many words I could use to describe the food served here, but this is a family newspaper and none of them should be available before the watershed. I can't deny my disappointment because the remaining candidates – 'awful', 'calamitous', 'the horror, the horror' – don't quite do it justice without the visceral attack of the expletive. Perhaps you could add a few in as you read. One between every word should do the job.

Divo, which occupies a once-imposing space at the southern end of Regent Street, is a very special kind of disaster; the sort Hollywood used to make films about in the 1970s. The decor is a disastrous mixture of overblown kitsch – swirly carpets and drapes that Middle Eastern dignitaries might favour for photo opportunities – and a down-home babushka, cottage look. It's as if two completely different teams from *Changing Rooms* have been let loose, armed only with half a million quid each of someone else's money, a bucketful of crystal meth and a taste bypass.

More disastrous than that are the poor, sweet waitresses' cherry-red outfits: lace-up bodice up top, a two-length skirt down below, so that it resembles a mumsy apron on one side and something so short on the other you worry they might catch a chill. One dining room is brightly lit, the other gloomy. If you go – perhaps because you are in the grips of a terminal illness and need a laugh – I recommend the latter. That way you won't have to look at the food as well as taste it.

The menu is long and overpriced and the three-figure caviar dishes are only the half of it. Fourteen pounds is an awful lot of money for pickles. It's an outrage for sloppy, limp strips of cucumber, huge peeled plum tomatoes and a couple of slices of mushy pear. One part of the menu, described as 'Divo Specials', lists dishes which 'were traditionally served to visiting dignitaries and the nobility of the Ukraine'. I can only assume Ukrainians have a healthy disdain for their dignitaries.

Top of the list is the 'Cossack Pork Sausage', and I am here to tell you that any comedic value obtained from the innuendo in that name was completely trounced by the appearance of the dish itself. The lengths of gnarled, under-seasoned gristly sausage arrived atop a lattice covering a ceramic bowl, which held a reservoir of burning liquor. Heaped on the sausage were crisp onion rings, which were immediately ignited by the flames from below. 'Now you blow it out,' the waitress said, her anxiety rising with the plumes of smoke. 'Now, please! Now!' This was the Red Army's scorched-earth policy realized in food. My companion, Amanda, is a game girl. Not only did she blow out the flames. She tasted the food as well. As a result she knows what carbonized onions taste like. They taste like charcoal.

I had 'Grandmother's Goluzbi', which sounds like an ailment of old age and ate like it too: floppy white cabbage leaves, wrapped around under-seasoned pork mince beneath a gloopy tomato sauce. I wish Grandma well. No matter. Here comes the main course, the venerable chicken kiev, and surely they can't bugger that up? 'Ah,' said Amanda, as it landed before us. 'Mum's gone to Iceland.' And it did indeed have that uniform breadcrumb shell-like-armour-plating look of the mass-produced item, which is amazing given they must have made it themselves. It was like the Belgian plain: dull and featureless. Two hockey-puck rabbit 'burgers' rolled in oats and served with half-melted lumps of a Red Leicester-type cheese, were as bad as they sound. Though not quite as bad as a side dish of 'buckwheat with fried onions and lard'. It had a weird plastic flavour which reminded me of the taste you get when you blow up a new lilo. This is not a good thing in a plate of food.

We finished – and I use that term loosely, for we did not finish anything – with a grim slice of cherry cheese-cake topped with a layer of jelly so solid you could have used it to culture bacteria in a Petri dish. The other dessert was a curl of cold pancake, buried beneath more sodden cherries. The pancake tasted like it had been made earlier in the day. In short, a load of old crêpe. The wine list is priced with oligarchs in mind, though it does include a Ukrainian Merlot at £17. Somehow I don't think the Ukraine is likely to be named the next great wine country. We checked the alcohol content. Somewhere between 'io to 13 per cent' it said. Ach. It's only wine.

Apparently 'Divo' is Ukrainian for 'amazing', a name I cannot argue with. It is amazing that anybody thought a restaurant like this would be a good idea, amazing that they invested a reputed £2 million in the conversion, amazing that what they bought with their money is so staggeringly, comically, bowel-twistingly poor. As we left, I was overcome by a strong feeling of gratitude, and not merely because the meal was over. I felt grateful to my great-grandfather Josef Boruchowicz. He was the one who had the gumption to escape the region of Eastern Europe that has supplied Divo's inspiration. He was the one who gave the finger to the Cossack horde and their dreadful pork sausage, who saved me from having to eat this stuff every day. Thank you, Josef. I owe you.

Despite lots of glowing five-star write-ups from people with Slavic names on restaurant websites, Divo appears, bizarrely, to have shut down. Clearly it will be missed. Just not by me.

Summer 1999

Elijah's Garden, 47a Goldhawk Road, London W12. Telephone: 020 8742 9286. Meal for two, including drinks and service, £18.

A few years ago, in pursuit of truth, I ate lunch in a Munich Bierkeller with a Nazi. You might think this an unlikely choice of both venue and lunch guest for a Jew, and you would be right. If I had been in restaurant-critic mode at the time I would have taken note of the food and might therefore be able to tell you now that my companion, the Nazi, had a rather agreeable schnitzel washed down by a playful bottle of Riesling. However, I was there less for the food (solid, Teutonic stuff, with the emphasis on roast meat and mashed potatoes, as you ask) than the politics. He was the scary kind of modern Nazi, a charismatic young chap in a well-cut suit who described himself as a marketing man for National Socialism. He told me that the Jews were the scum of the earth who must be expelled from Europe and that the Holocaust was an invention. I told him, as gently as I could, that I thought he was deranged. And then we ordered coffee.

In an effort to be crowned the hardest, most fearless restaurant critic in Britain I decided the time had come to reprise my Munich Bierkeller experience. The plan had been to mark this weekend's Notting Hill Carnival by visiting a restaurant representative of Afro-Caribbean cuisine. My editor thought I should try Elijah's Garden on the Goldhawk Road in Shepherd's Bush, which he had never visited but which he thought would fit the bill. He was wrong. Elijah's Garden is representative of nothing but itself. This is because it is owned and run by the Nation of Islam, a black separatist group which is to race relations what Concorde at full throttle is to silence. Their leader, the now ailing Louis Farrakhan, once described Judaism as 'a gutter religion' and said that Hitler had the right idea, for which views he has been barred from entering Britain.

Nevertheless the Nation prospers here and its bow-tied and besuited members can regularly be found selling its newspaper, the *Final Call*, on street corners across Britain's cities. Elijah's Garden serves as a meeting place for the Nation but they do still welcome ordinary punters through the door. I may be Jewish, part of that famous gutter religion, but I can still be an ordinary punter. I was accompanied by Abdul, a black journalist who has written much about the Nation and who reassured me that this really wasn't a risky venture. 'It will be fine,' he said. 'It's not like me trying to go to a Ku Klux Klan barbecue.'

He was right. We were greeted by an intense chap, wearing little round, steel-rimmed glasses and dressed entirely in chef's whites, who was welcoming in a rather stiff, formal way. It turned out he was the entire staff: chef, waiter, everything. Forties jazz played, the sounds of Ella and Billy floating through the small, square space. A couple of people were seated near the front window, by a table stacked with copies of the *Final Call*, but apart from that the place was empty. Eventually they would depart to leave us completely on our own.

The room is almost entirely white – white tiled floor, white walls, white ceilings – with small details like dado rails and coving picked out in gold paint. According to a friend of Abdul's, who once interviewed Farrakhan, the leader's house in Chicago is also decorated in this style, as are the Nation's places of worship. Funnily enough this white-and-gold thing is also the decor favoured for their bathrooms by Jewish families in Stanmore. I decided not to mention this to the waiter.

Abdul asked if he could smoke and was told sharply: 'We do not permit it.' We considered asking whether they served alcohol but decided not to. Clearly they didn't permit that either. Our waiter brought us the menu. It was written in black felt-tip on a piece of lined notepaper fastened to a clipboard. The sign outside describes Elijah's Garden as a 'Respect for life restaurant and take away'. It immediately became clear that this extended to the food, which is entirely vegetarian. All thoughts of jerk chicken and grilled snapper were banished.

As we worked our way through the choices our waiter kept repeating the dishes back to us, as if to suggest that he didn't think we quite understood the menu. We asked if we had ordered enough. He said sternly: 'It's your prerogative. You are the guests.' We felt empowered. We had been given the right to self-definition. Thus strengthened, we boldly ordered a glass of apple juice and a glass of orange juice. It was, after all, our prerogative. Portraits of Louis Farrakhan grinned down at us from the walls, approvingly.

For starters I ordered a bowl of their bean soup, which was pleasant in a homey sort of way. It was a deep rust colour, like a thick daal, and spiky with caraway and cumin. After this promising start everything went downhill, to such a degree that attempting a formal review of the food would not only be pointless but unfair. An example: Abdul's starter was described as a 'Pizza Petite'. This was one side of a piece of wholemeal pitta bread, layered with cheap, waxy Cheddar cheese, with a few slices of raw tomato and onion, all of which had then been flashed under the grill. In other words, the kind of food students make when there's nothing else left in the fridge.

Our two main courses were essentially the same thing: a soft, sweetish stew of vegetables, stuffed inside pitta bread in my case, under a layer of that same waxy cheese as in Abdul's starter. So, all in all, a pretty sad affair, but grist to my mill; after all, it is far better to attack anti-Semites for their lack of culinary skill than to even bother discussing their politics. (The Nazis? Pah! Worst strudel in Europe.) The best one can say about the food at Elijah's Garden is that it is probably the kind of stuff you really want to eat after a two-hour political meeting assigning competing creeds and religions to the gutter. It was also exceptionally cheap, at £18 for two including service.

Elijah's Garden is no more. Sadly, the same cannot be said for the Nation of Islam.

3
How the mighty are fallen

May 2009

Marco Pierre White Steakhouse and Grill, 109–117
Middlesex Street, London E1. Telephone: 020 7247 5050.
Meal for two, including wine and service, £120.

If you have the stomach for it, look up to the top of the
page and you will see a picture of me. It was taken within
the past year and displays the evidence of my midlife cri-
sis expressed through the medium of hair. I could, of
course, use a picture of myself from my early twenties
when, I realize now, I boasted the not unappealing bloom
of youth, but who the hell would I be kidding? Now let's
look at the menu for the Marco Pierre White Steakhouse
and Grill. There, on the back, in moody black and white,
is a picture of the man himself, all long flowing locks and
open-mouthed pout, the chef as rock god. It dates from,
ooh, 1989?

He doesn't look like that now. (People say he looks like
me now, the poor bastard; wicked sense of humour, that
Mother Nature.) So why is that picture there? Would it
be beyond absurd to suggest it is an attempt to trade on
old glories, those caviar- and oyster-kissed days long
before we had even heard of Gordon and Heston and all
the rest, when three-star Marco reigned supreme? Would

it? Heaven forfend. Instead I like to think he is offering it as a service to the diners in this restaurant. Because, once you have finished your meal, you can take home a copy of the menu and then throw darts at the face of the man responsible. It will give you far more satisfaction than any other part of the experience offered here.

The MPW Steakhouse and Grill, formerly Lanes, is a big, airy, pale-cream space, at the heart of the City, and sells food aimed at red-blooded hedge-fund managers who are down to their last million and crying for Nursie. The menu has a chummy handwritten script, but that is the only chummy thing about it, for almost everything we ate was awful in that 'someone must be punished' sort of way. We are deep into the glorious asparagus season now, so there was no excuse for the tasteless, woody, undercooked examples with a dull hollandaise sauce served here for £9.50. There is no excuse at any time of year for a kipper and whisky pâté (yes, I know; it sounds horrid. That's why I ordered it). It was served brutally fridge-cold, had the texture of chilled butter, and tasted of salt and smoke and little else. The advertised melba toast were two stupidly fragile sheets of something brown and lacy which were so thin I could check my watch through them (a pity; it reminded me lunch had only just begun).

At the heart of the mains is a list of steaks, either rib-eyes or fillets in various sizes and prices rising from late teens to close to £30. There are a number of preparations, including 'porcini rubbed'. We had to order that if only to find out what effect rubbing a mushroom against a steak has. There are some men in the City of London who might regard that as foreplay, but in gastronomic terms the answer is: none at all. It was a thin, feeble cut of meat, drenched in sticky jus, which bore no sign of the grill. Indeed, the uniformly crisped exterior was bizarre, an effect that might only be achieved at home by dropping the meat in the deep-fat fryer. God knows how they achieved it here.

I ordered the special of the day, the Lancashire hotpot, which was only special in the way Benny from *Crossroads* might once have been described as 'special'. Given Pierre White's Yorkshire roots, it could be enough to restart the Wars of the Roses. In a tiny bowl was dumped a pile of greasy lamb stew, leaking yellow oil, over the top of which were laid slices of undercooked potato that had been browned. It cost a shameful £12.50. The cauliflower in a cauliflower cheese was undercooked, the buttered peas dull and not very buttery.

At dessert there is only one 'choice' each day, in this case a bread-and-butter pudding, which, being soft and light, was the best thing we ate. It would have been even better if they had warmed it properly. All this, with one glass of good wine, served in a miserable tiny glass, for £100.

Does Marco Pierre White actually cook here? Don't be silly. Indeed, working out exactly how he is involved with the restaurants with which he is associated is notoriously difficult. But it's his name above the door, his face on the menu, and so he's the one we should blame. And so I do. Hand me the darts.

According to the restaurant's website the asparagus are still on the menu but have dropped in price by a pound; there is no longer the option to have your steak rubbed with porcini; and

they now serve a selection of desserts each day, rather than just
one. Since this review was published, Marco Pierre White has
gone on to open a number of other branches of his steakhouse
chain, which operate successfully.

May 2003

Brian Turner Mayfair, Grosvenor Square, London W1.
Telephone: 020 7596 3444. Dinner for two, including wine
and service, £110.

Dr Robert Atkins, the king of the low-carbohydrate diet,
died a couple of weeks back, at a relatively youthful
seventy-two. What a perfect story to point up the menda-
city of the diet industry. For decades Atkins made a
fortune selling desperate souls on the idea that the secret
to a long, healthy life lay in the pages of his books. And
then what happens? One morning he slips on an icy Man-
hattan pavement, bangs his head, and a few days later
they're arranging the funeral. All of which proves that
the Fates have a very dark sense of humour, and that life
is far too random for it to be wasted on a faddish diet that
excludes great bread and pasta.

A good meal is a life-affirming experience, and if ever
there was a chap who looks like he should be able to
deliver one of those, it's Brian Turner. You know Brian:
that nice, bulky Yorkshireman off the telly. The one who
does *Ready Steady Cook* and all that other celeb-chef stuff.
Behind the showbiz CV, however, is another one full of
experience and Michelin stars at places like the Savoy and

the Capital and restaurants with his own name above the door. A new Turner venture, particularly one promising to champion bold and flavoursome British food, should be a winner.

That it isn't, that it's a dud, speaks volumes about the desperation that can set in at this level of the London restaurant business. A big name like Turner can't just set up a restaurant. He has to create an event. He has to bring on the dancing girls and the snake charmers, which artifice doesn't suit him. The problems here begin with the location, the Millennium Mayfair Hotel on London's Grosvenor Square, a mere grenade's throw away from the barricades and watch towers that now surround the American Embassy. It is a gloomy, hard-arsed spot, an impression not helped by the massive black flags outside bearing Turner's name. It makes it look as if the Four Horsemen of the Apocalypse have given up on all that eternal damnation stuff and gone into the catering business.

Maybe I am not far off the mark, for the first part of Brian Turner Mayfair, the bar, might well be what Dante had in mind when he imagined the Seventh Circle of Hell. It's like a 1970s Spanish gay disco but with none of the erotic charge: blank walls, fierce pinprick lighting, dismally grating house music, and a bloody barman who has no idea what a kir is, let alone how to mix a good one. Thank God he had a friend to show him. I cannot for a moment imagine a mature chap like Brian Turner wishing to drink in this bar, and that's the problem. It is in no way a reflection of the man upon whom it is all being sold.

Onwards into the dining room, which is a cooler affair of white walls and raised platforms, divided by screens. It is big on glassware and much like the moon – which is to say, it has no atmosphere. It would help if the reception telephone didn't seem to ring loudly in every corner and if they cranked down the music. I also got little buzz out of seeing Turner himself, in pristine chef's whites holding not a single sauce stain, constantly wandering around the tables. I suppose I expected him to be doing the cooking, what with his name on those flags and all. Silly me.

And so to the food, the tone of which was set by a taster of two little deep-fried whitebait. Fine. Whitebait are a good British dish. But why tell us they have been crusted with coconut? In what way is that an improvement? I have no idea, because we couldn't taste the coconut at all. My first course was another bit of innovation, black pudding spring rolls with chilli plum sauce. I will be honest. I ordered these specifically because they sounded awful. I gain no satisfaction from the fact that they were, the black pudding sodden from the oil soaked up by the pastry in deep-frying. My companion, Toby, started with smoked eel, streaky bacon and warm potato salad, which was better but not great, and at this level and this price (£8.50) it should be great. The potato was a touch undercooked.

Indeed, the best we got out of this meal was adequate, as in a main course of grilled veal chop with chipolatas, lardons, button onions and mustard mash. It did the job, but we could both come up with other places which could do it better. My Lincolnshire duckling was well roasted – particularly the breast – but the accompanying pear and apricot stuffing was a solid lump of stodge. I can't list the other things on the plate because I can't recall them and I can't be fagged to look them up. Either they made an impression upon me or they didn't. And they didn't.

Toby finished with a white chocolate and raspberry trifle, which, to my taste, was too dainty an effort. The best part of the meal was my luscious fudge and blueberry bread-and-butter pudding, a superb carbohydrate overload which I ordered in memory of the good Dr Atkins. Service was swift but both edgy and nervous, as if they all thought a storm was approaching. And the bill for this with a £25 bottle of Rioja was £110. It is a lot of money for an experience that flirted only with adequacy and was occasionally on nodding terms with awful. Be warned.

Since this review was published I have run into Brian Turner on a number of occasions. He has not once complained about what I said, and has been unfailingly polite. He closed Brian Turner Mayfair in 2008.

May 2003

Petrus, the Berkeley Hotel, Wilton Place, London SW1. Telephone: 020 7235 1200. Dinner for two, including wine and service, £150.

It is a curious fish dish that encourages the maître d', on hearing you order it, to announce: 'I am Belgian and in

Belgium this is not how we cook turbot.' My dear, this is not how they cook turbot anywhere. The menu description said: 'Braised turbot with Welsh rarebit glaze, smoked cod roe with aubergine caviar and sautéed baby gem lettuce, lemon-grass velouté'. The maître d' described the dish to me, just as it was written. He said something like: 'I wanted you to know how complex it is,' and wandered away. My wife, Pat, watched him go and said: 'That sounded like he was trying to dissuade you from ordering it.'

Perhaps he was nervous. The reopening of Marcus Wareing's flagship restaurant Petrus at the Berkeley Hotel in London's Knightsbridge is a big deal, most of all for Marcus Wareing. It is no secret that the chef, a protégé of Gordon Ramsay, was dismayed not to be upgraded from one to two Michelin stars at the old site in St James's. The new premises are supposed to provide him with a launch pad from which to reach those stars.

I should say that I, too, was surprised the old Petrus didn't get upgraded. Wareing is a gifted and unashamedly bourgeois chef, who is not scared of big flavours. I still have taste memories of his dishes: of seared scallops in a lobster bisque tasting ripely of the sea, for example, or his sweet, glazed round of pork belly. More recently, at the Savoy Grill, he showed an understanding of classy simplicity. Here, though, simplicity has gone out of the over-gilded window. It's not just bells and whistles. It's the whole damn percussion section of the London Symphony Orchestra. And not all the instruments are playing the same tune.

First though, the good things. The new room, until

recently La Tante Claire, is a huge improvement on the old Petrus, which felt like a place you went to be interred rather than fed. The walls have been padded in a warm shade of claret and the old formal service, which made it feel as if there were a party of bishops on table seven, has given way to something brisk, light and jolly. The giddy, theatrical turn of the many trolleys – for champagne and wine, for cheese and sweets – adds to the drama.

Top marks must also go to the sommelier, Alan Holmes, for creating a truly democratic list. Yes, there are some of the most expensive wines known to humanity. A 1928 Chateau Petrus, perhaps? Yours for £11,600. But the list also starts with a 'Sommelier's selection' of twenty-four wines. All are under £20 and the cheapest costs £14.50, which immediately gets the punters on their side. We chose a Lebanese Hochar Rouge from the makers of Chateau Musar, and it was gorgeous. Every top-flight restaurant in London should have a list like this.

They won't be wanting the menu, though. It is expensive, at £55 for three courses, but that is of a piece with other London restaurants at the level to which Petrus aspires. There are, however, supplements, which look purely opportunistic. At the Square, which already has two Michelin stars, grouse costs £5 extra, around the price of the raw ingredient. Here it costs an inexcusable £12.

More important is the quality this big money buys. Not everything we ate was bad. As a taster we were served a shot glass of gazpacho, unnecessarily sweetened with pineapple. Pat is allergic to pineapple so she was brought instead a cup of hot, creamy, white onion soup. Wareing does these truffled soups spectacularly well, as this one proved yet again. She also ordered the best main dish: 'Braised hare served with creamed Savoy cabbage, glazed red onions and a rich Madeira wine sauce'. It read well and it ate well. The meat came in an unctuous, tender cake, and it was intense with the flavour of field and autumn.

We were much less lucky elsewhere. Because I am here to serve you I ordered not according to appetite, but description. If a dish read badly I had to discover if it really was a disaster. So: 'Crispy chargrilled veal sweetbread, braised marrow with garlic and thyme, velouté infused with Amaretto and almonds'. The sauce was so sweet it should have come with a health warning from the British Dental Association. Afterwards I had the claggy-mouth feel one gets from drinking sweet, creamy cocktails in Essex. For the record, almonds had nothing to say to sweetbreads apart from: go away.

A starter of over-spiced scallops with a potato salad, artichokes and truffled cream was again a collection of ingredients that made little sense together on the plate. It was not a patch on Wareing's old way with scallops. And then that turbot, with the cacophony of smoked cod roe and spiced aubergine, Welsh rarebit and, lord help us, the lemon-grass velouté. The dish made me ponder the purpose of cooking at this level. It is, I think, about preparing the best produce so that they taste most intensely of themselves. Other ingredients on the plate must serve that cause. Here the fish was obliterated, partly by a very heavy hand on the salt, but mostly by the weird assemblage. Turbot is a noble fish. Leave the poor thing alone. I should, I suppose, have listened to the maître d'.

Here's the problem: Wareing is now actively cooking to get two or three Michelin stars, and it doesn't work that way. You just have to cook the way you cook, and if it's good the accolades will come. You have to be yourself. At the moment a lot of the cooking at Petrus is not good, Wareing isn't being himself – and it's a crying shame.

Wareing reacted curiously to this review, telling the then moderator of one of the online food discussion boards that I knew nothing about food. Apparently, that evening, when I ordered the much-pilloried turbot dish, he had replaced the lemon-grass velouté with a cep sauce, and I hadn't noticed. I responded later that it couldn't have been much of a cep sauce or I would have jumped to my feet shouting: 'Who put all the mushrooms in the lemon-grass velouté?' We eventually made friends again and, in 2006, during research for a book on high-end restaurants around the world, he told me that he 'got it wrong at the beginning. I went from driving an old banger to a Ferrari and lost control.' In 2007 Petrus won its second star and, a little after that, Marcus Wareing parted company with his one-time mentor Gordon Ramsay. The restaurant is now called Marcus Wareing at the Berkeley, and still holds two Michelin stars. In 2012 I published a generally very positive review of Marcus Wareing at the Berkeley in the London Magazine.

4
I must get out less:
Dispatches from Britain

June 2007

Carpe Diem, Millennium Parade, Explorer Lane, Harbour-side, Bristol. Telephone: 0117 3 169173. Meal for two, including wine and service, £90.

It seems the road to Bristol is paved with good intentions. The last time I came here it was also to review a restaurant with a loudly proclaimed ethical policy. Bordeaux Quay made much of its non-existent carbon footprint, its recycling systems and the way it sourced its ingredients locally. When I pointed out that it then used those locally sourced ingredients to make lousy dishes that had nothing to do with the locality from which they were sourced, I received endless emailed complaints which said the chef-proprietor, Barney Haughton, deserved to be canonized for what he had done for the environment. A bunch of these emails came from people with the surname Haughton. Well, if your family won't support you, who will?

I just hope the owners of Carpe Diem in Bristol do not have a multitude of family members with email accounts because it is, if anything, worse. The food is that nightmarish coincidence of really stupid ideas and grossly incompetent execution. In a year with some quite spectacular lows this is, by far, the lowest. Forget the road to Bristol. The food here is a journey down the road to culinary hell.

Like Bordeaux Quay, Carpe Diem is located in a shiny new development down by the waterside. It is a big, rectangular echoey space which, when empty, as it was on our visit, looks like a modern furniture shop. Like Bordeaux Quay it declares itself carbon and nitrates neutral. Everything that can be recycled is; all coffees and teas are Fairtrade; the bogs use a water-conservation system; and all meat comes from animals that are free range and – their words – 'live their life with dignity'.

Then they take that meat and treat it with so little respect, so little dignity, they might as well cut out the middleman – the poor, benighted diner – and shove it straight into the wormery. Take, for example, a starter of smoked duck, served sliced, fridge-cold, and with some of the clingfilm still attached. To go with this was a chunk of hard, crumbly chocolate torte. Is it a witty, interesting and modern food combination? No. It is horrible, pointless and idiotic one. There was also a gingerbread crisp that didn't taste of ginger and a quenelle of quince raisin compote which was merely a poor man's Branston. These ingredients occupied four separate corners of a plate like guests at a party who didn't want to be introduced, and rightly so.

There was a similar plating for a grossly over-seasoned crab cake which tasted not at all of crab, with pickled fennel that had no aniseed kick, and some gluey caramelized kumquat that reminded me of orange squash syrup. Amazingly the mains were, if anything, worse. Fillets of sea bass, at a shameful £17.50, had been fried for so long they had soaked up all the fat, managing to be both dry and greasy at the same time. They sat on a mess of blackened and crushed potatoes with red onions and capers, and around that was a split beurre blanc; in short, a puddle of slightly stale clarified butter.

I ordered my main course because it read like a car crash. This was a motorway pile-up: Cotswold Old Spot tenderloin pork with lemon, liquorices, pumpkin and café au lait. On the upside all I could taste of those silly ingredients in the tiny splatter of sauce was a sweetened medicinal bitterness. On the downside I could taste nothing in the pork. It was overcooked in a way that made it irrelevant whether the meat had come from an animal that had lived its life in a Cotswolds idyll or an industrial pig shed in Droitwich. So much for ethical principles: this was a disgraceful waste of a fine animal. We also tried a side dish of their mushroom ragout: a plate of hot-but-not-cooked button mushrooms slathered in something akin to tomato purée.

The most successful dish of the day, in the sense that it was merely mediocre rather than horrid, was a lemon tart with no citrus zing, made with pastry that was soggy and almost as thick as my mobile phone. I ordered the 'double' vanilla crème brûlée. I have no idea what the double thing was about. I do know the crème had split. It was a pot of sweetened scrambled egg. I pointed this out and they took it off the bill. Even so, with just two glasses of wine, that bill came to £80.

I am genuinely baffled. I do not understand why restaurateurs who would go to such trouble to get their ethical policies in order would then allow such dismal food to emerge from the kitchen. For the record, if you want good food served in a restaurant with a smart ethical policy, visit Acorn House, in London's King's Cross, which was named best newcomer in this year's *OFM* awards. As for Carpe Diem, if you should ever be so unfortunate as to find yourself there, do what the name says: seize the day and get out of there as fast as you can.

Carpe Diem did not seize the day. It closed. Bordeaux Quay is very much still in business and has won many awards.

November 2003

Drumbeg Hotel and Seafood Restaurant, Drumbeg, by Lochinver, Sutherland. Telephone: 01571 833236. Meal for two, including wine and service, £75.

I will remember only one thing of my trip to the Drumbeg Hotel and Seafood Restaurant in the Scottish Highlands and it is this: hunger; pit-of-the-stomach, hand-trembling hunger. This is never a good recommendation for a restaurant. The American food writer Jeffrey Steingarten once said that he has not been hungry since 1974. Until I went to Drumbeg I was with him.

It was not meant to be this way. I decided to go there because of the menu they sent me. It read so beautifully I immediately wanted to be eating from it. It said things like: 'A plate of local Drumbeg chanterelles' and 'creel-caught langoustines with mayonnaise'. It was all about the best ingredients – bountiful in the Highlands – simply prepared. It was a menu of great virtues and it seemed reasonable that I should make the effort to get there. Drumbeg was the original reason for the trip that took me eventually to the marvellous Summer Isles Hotel described here recently and required the same flight to Inverness and then a long drive to the very northern edge of the Assynt peninsula, to that bit of the map just before the sea starts flowing over the edge of the world.

I missed lunch on the plane but decided that, rather than stop, I would make straight for Drumbeg and its culinary promise. Over two and half hours of mad driving later, through spectacular scenery, I arrived at the sombre, grey-rendered building with its beautiful view of Loch Drumbeg. As I signed in I said to the woman present, who was one of the owners: 'Any chance of a sandwich? I missed lunch, you see, and . . .' She looked at me as if I'd made an indecent proposal. 'Oh, no. The kitchen is closed. We're a small hotel. We can't do you a sandwich.' Really? Nothing? 'Well, I might be able to find you a dry oatcake.'

It wasn't just the lack of hospitality that grated. It was the sneer that went with it. Come round to my house and I can run you up a bloody sandwich. I might even do better than that. Perhaps she saw my hand trembling, for she dug me out a couple of tiny biscuits, but delivered them with such ill-grace I felt embarrassed eating them. Certainly it was not enough to bridge the gap. By the time dinner came round I was starving, and this is no way to order; decisions in restaurants should never be driven by the physical imperative of survival.

So, what is there to tell you? The ingredients at Drumbeg, once you get to eat them, are as good as they sounded and as good as they should be, but there really is a dismal parsimony to the whole operation. A plate of five different charcuterie sounds good value at £4.80, but is less so when you get only one mingy slice of four of them. The seafood platter – five langoustines, five squat lobsters, five oysters, one brown and one velvet crab and half a small lobster for £25.95 – was a sight to behold. But is it reasonable to charge another £2.90 for a side salad, and did you really have to look so put out when I asked for extra mayonnaise? For the record, breakfast next morning continued the theme: it presented the saddest sausage I have seen in a long time.

The view from the dining room over the loch is gorgeous, but when dusk has fallen you are left with the dining room itself, which is a grey space with all the charm of a dentist's waiting room without the promise of anaesthetic. The bedrooms, at £50 a night, are suburban-semi chic. I know what the owners will be saying this morning: that they are a small operation in the middle of nowhere. Sure you are. But you are also charging people to come and stay. The word 'hotel' is above the door. That places certain responsibilities upon your shoulders, and if you can't meet those responsibilities then stop trying to entice people up to see you. Drumbeg is too far to go for hunger.

The owners of the Drumbeg Hotel and Seafood Restaurant were not especially happy with this review. They wrote to the Observer complaining that if you googled the word 'Drumbeg' the first thing that came up was my review. 'We respect Mr Rayner's views,' they said in a letter to the paper, adding 'they are not shared by all (see the independent, non-fee-paying guides like the Time Out Eating and Drinking Guide, Good Hotel Guide, Which? Guide to Good Hotels, Scotland the Best, Michelin, The Rough Guide to Scotland, etc.). Unfortunately for us, none of these reviews features on Google which makes it even worse.' They asked the Observer to remove the review from the website, which the paper declined to do, explaining that they never remove articles from the site unless there is a legal reason for doing so. The Drumbeg Hotel and Seafood restaurant closed shortly after. However, a small hotel called Blar na Leisg at Drumbeg House has since set up near by, is going strong, and in no way should be confused with the hotel I reviewed.

August 2009

The Rajput, 9–11 Cheltenham Parade, Harrogate. Telephone: 01423 562113. Meal for two, including wine and service, £55.

It is common to describe a dreadful restaurant meal as being like a motorway pile-up. After dinner at the Rajput in Harrogate I have realized the comparison is entirely wrong; at least with a motorway accident the emergency services eventually come to deal with the pain and distress. With a terrible restaurant experience no one ever comes. You are left only with the bill and the after-taste and an abiding sense that you did something really stupid by booking a table.

Perhaps I did, but my motives were pure. A year or two back I was contacted by Shaan Khan, the chef of the Rajput, who told me he was the Indian Jamie Oliver. Let's leave all the mean jokes at Saint Jamie's expense to one side and assume Shaan meant he was a young, inventive no-nonsense cook, bursting with charisma, who could inspire an audience with his Indian food. There's nothing wrong with that.

Which is more than I can say for his restaurant, a low-ceilinged space, full of heavy-footed, carved wooden furniture, and heavy-footed waiters, exuding an air of mild panic. Maybe they knew what was coming. The service was that special kind of bad, the type that slips easily into hilarious without ever quite going through infuriating. One waiter speaks almost no English but insisted on coming to look at us and take orders that never arrived. We asked for a pint of Kingfisher. We did that a number of times. He nodded. He smiled. He went away. It took ten minutes and another waiter to tell us they don't have it in pints, only bottles. We ordered three starters. Only when the first two had arrived were we told the third, the lamb chops, was off. A menu was jabbed under our nose. 'Choose something else. Have the chicken tikka masala.' We did as we were told. It never arrived. Of course the original lamb chops were still on the bill at the end. Much of the food took an age to turn up. When it did, we regretted the fact.

Among the starters was a dish called 'Aubergine

Delight'. See that word on a menu and you know it won't be. In this case it was spiced aubergine under an avalanche of cheap melted cheese, swimming with oil. It was like a leftover dish the original of which had never been sighted. A mixed plate of starters – a doughy bhaji, a curious vegetable samosa containing sweetcorn, the last remaining gnarly undercooked lamb chop in Harrogate which they'd managed to find for us – was merely mediocre, an attempt perhaps to lull us into a false sense of security before the main courses.

But then we should have seen the danger coming from the menu descriptions. Shaan's 'Satay Twist' was, as the words said, pieces of chicken rolled in peanut butter and served in a slick of a honey and chilli sauce. As the words didn't say, it was so sweet it made you want to stick your tongue out and bite into it, in an attempt to get some feeling back in. Scariest of all, that paragraph on the menu began with the words, 'I did it again!' What do you mean, Shaan? That you keep doing things like this? Really? In the name of God, stop. Worse still was the lamb pepper masala, described as a 'Rajput twist on a classic French dish', the twist being it was astonishingly horrible, the overload of pepper in the pond of beige sauce adding a tang of urea to it. Incidentally, I have absolutely no idea what the classic French dish it was meant to be referencing was.

A king prawn makhanwala was sold with the optimistic legend: 'Go on, don't be shy, lovely jubbly.' No, it wasn't. A bath with randy scorpions would have been lovelier than this. It was a bunch of king prawns drowned in a lake of something the colour of Sunny Delight, only with none of the subtlety or grace notes. It was sweet and sickly and violent. A braised lamb dish was saved from being OK by the addition of a pile of cold, greasy fried onions. At £110 for four none of this was cheap. The one bright spot was the wine list, which listed a bottle of 2006 Hugel Gewürztraminer, a truly fabulous wine, at an astonishing £15.95, which isn't far off retail. But of course, this being the Rajput, they only had one bottle left, and half of that had already been drunk. We got a couple of glasses out of it, the high point of the meal. It was all downhill from there. And at the end, the emergency services never came.

It turned out I was wrong. The emergency services did eventually come. Shaan Khan, his brother Raza and mother, Paveen, were arrested, charged, tried and eventually convicted of people trafficking. In 2010 they were found guilty of bringing nine men to the UK from India and Pakistan, confiscating their passports and forcing them to work for very low wages. It made me feel guilty about the brutal words I had saved for the quality of the service. No wonder they weren't doing a good job. They were being abused. 'These people had come over to the country, expecting to get a good job and a good life while working legitimately,' a spokesman for the Borders Agency said, 'but they found themselves essentially entrapped into working in conditions they were unhappy with and their passports being removed, doctored or destroyed. That very much undermines both immigration control and the safety of people who have got every right to come here to work legitimately.' The brothers were sentenced to three years in prison. The Rajput, unsurprisingly, is no more. It has been replaced by an entirely different Indian restaurant under new ownership.

5

On the high street

June 2003

McDonald's, various branches. Meal for two, £8.

This review is as much an act of solidarity as criticism. Last month the leading Italian restaurant critic, Edoardo Raspelli, was sued for £15 million by McDonald's, after he described their hamburgers as 'rubbery' and said their chips tasted like 'cardboard'. Its product, he said, was 'gastronomically repellent'. Nothing wrong there, you might say. And yet we must never assume. I have, of course, eaten at McDonald's. (I have done a lot of things of which I am not proud.) But the last time was long ago, and I was using the place for its only unarguable purpose: as a sudden source of food energy when nothing else was on offer. The time had come for another visit.

I went to a branch close to my home. Do I need to describe it? Do I need to tell you about the slumped, resigned shoulders of the poor buggers working there? No? Good. I started with a classic: the Big Mac. This I deconstructed. First I put the slimy grey puck of a burger into my mouth and, yes, Mr Raspelli, it is indeed rubbery, but so much worse than that. The thing leaked hot, greasy, salty water into my mouth. Next the bun, whose third ingredient after flour and water is sugar. It was floppy and burnt. Finally, there was a vicious bile-esque back-taste to the sauce.

So far, so disgusting. On to the chips. Cardboard, yes, but fatty cardboard, and after half a minute any crispness sagged away. Next I tried one of the new dishes recently introduced as part of their 'Ever Changing New Tastes' campaign. 'Chicken Selects' are breaded strips of chicken breast, and are a truly remarkable example of fast-food science. Although they are clearly pieces of breast, they taste of chicken not at all. They taste of salt. And then, the worst item of all, a pasta and feta cheese salad in a lemon and olive oil dressing. After this one I needed counselling: floppy pasta, cheese like chalk dust, and a syrupy dressing packed with sugar. I studied the ingredients. In the olive oil dressing glucose syrup comes ahead of the oil. I only ate this because I was being paid to do so. The salad contains sweetcorn. It was that bad.

Was there anything that was passable? Yes. I quite liked the berry and yoghurt crunch. The yoghurt was sharp and there was real fruit in the berry mixture. So, what have we learned? Not much. McDonald's food is a culinary disaster, but then we knew this. It's also cheap and fun for kids in (extreme) moderation. But for the company to be furious when a restaurant critic tells the truth is like a hooker reacting with outrage at being called loose. It's fair comment. McDonald's may fume. They may even consider reaching for their lawyers, to which I say only this: come and have a go if you think you're hard enough. I stand by every word.

McDonald's in the UK took absolutely no action against me. The Italian judge in Mr Raspelli's case instructed the two parties to come to terms outside the court. Since then nothing has been heard of the case. However, as a result of the legal action, his criticisms of McDonald's have been repeated many, many times.

November 2010

Aberdeen Angus Steakhouse, 4–6 Garrick Street, London WC2 (and nine other locations). Telephone: 020 7379 0412. Meal for two, including wine and service, £100.

Blimey. Branches of the Aberdeen Angus Steakhouse chain have had a makeover. It's like seeing Waynetta Slob in Gucci. Not real Gucci, mind; the tacky knock-off stuff that you'd buy in Bodrum market on your Turkish summer holidays. There is overly clean, dark-wood panelling, bare brick of the sort used to build new bungalows on the outskirts of Swindon, and a continuous line of red neon around the top of the walls which casts the room in the sort of glow I last saw in Amsterdam behind a big picture window framing a woman in her pants who was for hire. Am I selling it to you? Am I?

Of course we cannot assume on looks alone. Or, to be more precise, I can't just assume it's a nightmare without having eaten there. Having done so, here's what I can say. It's a nightmare; the sort that has you awakening with the bed sheets bunched in your hands. Not everything was appalling. The 10 oz rib eye was fine: not without flavour, not tough, served medium rare, as asked. Likewise the service, by a nice Hungarian chap, was good. He's wasted here.

But that good steak set everything else into relief. A starter sharing platter brought rings of deep-fried calamari with all the texture and flavour of surgical support hose. A bolus of breaded chicken breast was desperate and dry, skewers of prawns simply odd. Spareribs were the colour of an old lady's velour sofa and edible, in the sense that I ate them. This cost the best part of £15, the best part being £14.95. That's the point. Aberdeen Angus Steakhouses are not cheap. We had one glass of wine, one dessert, and ran up a bill of over £90. Even the rib eye doesn't make that acceptable. The New York strip was dense, flavourless and unrested. Why import your beef all the way from Argentina – feel the carbon footprint – simply to do this to it?

Worse were the béarnaise and peppercorn sauces, which were possibly the nastiest things I've put in my mouth since a game of Truth or Dare at college (don't ask). We must assume they made them from scratch, which makes the fact they tasted like they had been reconstituted from powder all the more remarkable. The peppercorn sauce, in particular, was vile. It looked like the sort of thing you might extract from a long-untended wound. You could achieve the effect of their onion rings at home by opening a bag from the freezer. Chips, unforgivably, were lukewarm and flaccid. A lemon meringue pie had cold, soggy pastry. I have long wondered how these places stay in business; have wanted to run in to naive tourists who have unwittingly taken seats in there and bellow: 'Save yourselves!' No amount of polished wood panelling or red neon changes any of that.

Even the Wikipedia entry for the Aberdeen Angus Steakhouse group has a section dedicated to their reputation and the fact that journalists have written regularly of how just how poor the food and decor are. In March 2011 the comedian David Mitchell suggested in his Observer newspaper column that the British government ought to apply to Unesco for world heritage site status for the restaurant chain for their 'proud heritage of serving shoe leather with béarnaise sauce to neon-addled out-of-towners'.

6

Money can't buy you love . . .
or nice things to eat

October 2011

Le Caprice, Arlington Street, London SW1. Telephone: 020 7629 2239. Meal for two, including service, £120.

Don't go to Le Caprice hungry. After my experience there, I am minded to wonder why anybody goes there at all. But certainly don't go there eager to be fed. It was a Saturday night, and to my astonishment I had managed to book a table for four people at 9 p.m. without pulling strings. I didn't think this was possible. Le Caprice, the cornerstone of Richard Caring's Caprice Holdings group, which also owns the Ivy, Scott's and J. Sheekey among others, has just celebrated its thirtieth birthday with a glossy makeover. It looks like an art deco ocean liner, all chrome panels and uplighters and friendly buzz. It is the ultimate insider joint; the sort of place where the diners are more famous than the people in the black-and-white photos hung on the wall. Cliff Richard eats there. What more does one need to say? Sir Cliff. Eats. There.

But I never had; it was clearly time to make amends. We arrived on the dot to find a packed dining room and a flustered front-of-house team who asked us to wait.

Just for a few minutes. And a few minutes more. And a couple more after that. The apologetic promises became more slippery as the minutes passed. At 9.15 p.m. we were finally led to our table. Now let's not pretend: they recognized me the moment I walked through the door. They know exactly what I do for a living and, from the fact I had booked under a pseudonym, knew I was there professionally. Which leads me to wonder, just how long would we have been left standing in that queue if they hadn't clocked me?

Menus arrived and with them a waiter who was to warmth and charm what Burma is to democracy. He was brusque, distracted, and at one point managed to break off from taking our order to have a sharp exchange of words over our heads with a junior colleague. We asked him for more butter to go with the bread we were scarfing to fend off hunger. The butter never arrived. We had to ask again. The menu at Le Caprice is long and slightly odd. There are comfort-food items here – fish cakes with sorrel sauce, for example, or fish and chips with crushed peas – alongside offerings of sashimi, duck salad with shiso or Thai-baked sea bass, as if they are trying to cater for people with self-consciously cosmopolitan tastes who can't be fagged to go out and find the real thing. Starters begin at £7 for a bowl of soup before hurling themselves into the teens; main courses pick up where the starters left off and head towards £30 and beyond.

Still, it was a list of things to eat and that had to be a good thing. We were, after all, hungry. Which was how we stayed for longer than could ever be strictly reasonable. A full fifty-five minutes after the time of our booking, with nothing on the table, and a brush-off from the front-of-house staff when we enquired – them: 'It's on its way'; me: 'Where from exactly?' – my party agreed that if we hadn't been served when a full hour was up, we would leave. The starters made it just two minutes before our self-imposed deadline.

It was a mixed old bag. The best of the lot was a lovely special of seared foie gras, cooked accurately on a thin, sticky, onion galette. And so it should have been lovely at £16. Good-quality seared scallops with crisp bacon and sweetcorn purée were overcooked. At £13, the squid and chorizo was an exceptionally mean little assembly, featuring fatty rather than meaty chorizo. An endive pear and radish salad was so underdressed as to inspire feverish debate as to whether there was anything on it at all; we had to ask for more dressing.

The main courses were not an improvement. The chips with the deep-fried fish looked anaemic. I tried one. Hot, raw potato. We sent them back. A portion two thirds the size of the original came back, properly cooked this time, but meagre. The fried fish was fine, if unexceptional. Calf's liver was cut thick and served pink and had a good smoky char. Best of the lot was the Caprice burger, a serious hockey puck of minced beef, served medium rare, as requested, and with good shoestring potatoes. Worst, by far, was £24 worth of completely under-seasoned plaice fillets with surf clams on a flavourless beurre blanc. It was nursery food, or food for people with insecure dentures.

I looked about the room. It was occupied by what I believe we're meant to call a senior crowd; the sort who might find such soft food helpful. I brought the average age down big time, which, given I'm forty-five, is saying something. It explained a lot. Presumably Le Caprice really was once marvellous, a place of reassuring virtues, which looked after its regulars properly. And so those regulars have stayed, not noticing what the passage of time has done to the dear old ocean liner they so adore. But here's the most peculiar thing. I regard Caprice Holdings as one of the most professional restaurant groups in the country. They are, rightly, famed for the level of service at places like Scott's and the Ivy; the food is unerringly reliable. Not ground-breaking perhaps, but reliable, which is what it has to be to justify the prices.

And yet this place, the one from which the company takes its name, is a shambles. And if even I can't get a good experience from Le Caprice, what hope is there for those unknown to the restaurant? The two desserts we had, an orange and almond cake with cardamom ice cream, and their famed iced berries with white chocolate sauce, were the best part of the meal. They felt like the sweeties children are sometimes given after enduring inoculations at the doctors. We had been brave. We had taken our punishment. And now we just wanted to go home.

In a Twitter exchange subsequent to the publication of this review, the late film-director-turned-restaurant-critic Michael Winner told me he had been going to Le Caprice for decades and had never had a bad meal there. I did not doubt him.

April 2011

Salloos, 62–64 Kinnerton Street, London SW1. Telephone: 020 7235 4444. Meal for two, including drinks and service, £170.

Kinnerton Street in Knightsbridge is one of those quiet London back lanes, shadow-dressed and narrow, where it is quite possible to imagine being separated from your money with menaces late at night. In many ways I would regard such an experience as preferable to eating at the fancy Pakistani restaurant Salloos, which occupies a mews house there. At least with a mugging it's over quickly and it doesn't leave a nasty taste in the mouth. However, the outcome – you will be left standing on the kerb with a lighter wallet and wondering what the hell you did to deserve it – will be the same.

Don't believe me? Go have a look at the website, a smart move for anybody considering eating out in London these days. Gasp at the prices: £15.90 for tandoori lamb chops, £12.90 for chicken ginger, £6.50 for a bowl of daal. Except it's so much worse than that, because the generous folk who run Salloos somehow forgot to update their menu with the current prices. Those lamb chops? They actually cost £24.50. For that sort of money I'd want the whole damn lamb to come out and sing me nursery rhymes. The chicken ginger is £17, the daal an extraordinary £10.50, the cost of the ingredients for which – a handful of lentils, a bit of onion, a few spices – can be measured in pence.

The problem for Salloos is that while what they do

used to be rare in London – a distinct Pakistani menu rather than the generic 'Indian' – today it is everywhere. There's the fast-growing Mirch Masala chain, the triumvirate of Lahore Kebab Houses, stand-out places like Needoo's Grill and, of course, the great Tayyabs on Fieldgate Street in Whitechapel, where lamb chops cost £6 and a bowl of daal is £5.20. I know the argument. All these restaurants may be great but they are rough and ready. It's all wipe-down menus and tables, and waiters with sharp elbows getting you in and getting you out.

This is true. Salloos is nothing like any of those. Enter through a cosy lounge bar area downstairs. You are then led upwards to a cool white dining room set into the roof space, decorated with a few bits of Asian art. I can well imagine Imran Khan schmoozing his girlfriends here. I have no problem with the notion that food from the Indian subcontinent can be grand rather than just bargain-basement high-street curry house; that there can be a serious, even thrilling expression of that food that can justify the big money. Anybody lucky enough to have experienced the great Vineet Bhatia's cooking at Rasoi Vineet Bhatia just off the King's Road – his home-smoked tandoori salmon, for example, or his sesame-crusted black daal roll – could hardly think otherwise. Blimey, but it's good. Likewise Benares, Tamarind, Veeraswamy and Amaya are all capable of delivering some very good food.

The food at Salloos isn't like that. It's awful. Perhaps it wasn't always like this. Perhaps back in the 1970s it was vibrant and fresh and thrilling. Now it is dull and clumsy. I have been known to travel large distances across London for serious tandoori lamb chops. They should be dark and crusted with spice, with a narrow ribbon of crisped fat at their backs, and just a hint of pink in the eye. You should be desperate to pick them up and rip every last tangle of meat from the bone. At Tayyabs – and forgive me, but it really is the benchmark – they come out still smoking on a cast-iron platter that has only just left the oven.

Here they arrive, cooling and dull on a stainless-steel plate with some tired salad. Not enough heat has been applied, so they are cooked through and tough, and not enough seasoning, so they are dull and insipid. They are tragic. Tandoori prawns, four largish ones at a fiver each, are no better. And then to the curry courses: a set of tiny bowls arrives containing a bunch of dun-coloured substances. They recall the old Jewish joke about the bad restaurant: the food was so lousy – and the portions, so small! We had ordered a curry of chicken and ginger, and another of stir-fried kidneys to mark the Pakistani love of offal. Amazingly it is very difficult to tell which is which. Both are one-note concoctions of salt and chilli and not much else.

Daal, though a simple dish, can be cooling and comforting, full of myriad strata of flavour. This is just so much beige. An aubergine curry is a little better – you can tell it's aubergine – but not by much. Breads are OK but have clearly been hanging about in the kitchen a little while. All of this is served with the ludicrous, outdated pomposity of silver service. Thrill to what a man can do with a spoon and a fork held in one hand, even though I'd be much happier serving myself.

The best course is dessert, a 'home-made' chocolate

amaretto ice cream, and a hyper-sweet halwa gajar, made of grated carrots, which arrives at the table emanating the sort of heat usually achieved by the use of a microwave. It is, of course, impossible to imagine that a restaurant charging prices like this would do such a thing. There is a loyal customer base who will take umbrage at all of this, people who have been coming for decades and who would regard the cheaper joints as far beneath them. They are the sort of people who worry more about the tablecloth than the food. In which case Salloos will suit them perfectly. As I left I was so appalled by the bill – they even have the cheek to impose a £1.50 cover charge just for sitting down – that I tweeted out a picture of it and asked my many restaurant-minded followers to name the restaurant. They listed all the high-end Indians in London. It was an hour or so before anybody named Salloos. It seems it has been forgotten. That strikes me as a good thing.

Shortly after this review was published, Salloos corrected the prices on their website to bring them into line with those on their menus.

April 2009

Time and Space, The Royal Institution, 21 Albemarle Street, London W1. Telephone: 020 7670 2956. Meal for two, including wine and service, £90.

I am always intrigued by the way clever people can have really stupid ideas. And so to the Royal Institution, that

venerable building on London's Albemarle Street which
has been a hotbed of scientific debate and promotion for
over two centuries. The place is rammed with people
thinking clever thoughts. Unfortunately it seems none of
them have anything to do with what might make for a
pleasant lunch. Not long ago they reopened the building
after a major refurbishment, which introduced zippy
panels in saturated colours, plasma screens, atriums and
a restaurant called Time and Space. If there is any justice
in this world a small black hole, a rip in the very fabric of
the time–space continuum, will soon open under Albemarle Street and put us all out of its misery.

It is a large, book-lined, rectangular room, with too
many glass entrances and exits, so that baffled elderly
people constantly wandered in and out from various corners looking for staff. It is a blessing they didn't always
find them, given the quality of the food here. Mind you,
even if you do get seated don't necessarily expect what
you have ordered to arrive swiftly or, perhaps, at all; those
books might well come in handy as a way of passing the
time. The service was a new and special kind of
cack-handedness, which could form the basis of one of
their famed Christmas lectures, entitled 'Lunch and How
Not to Do It'. There was the water poured on to the table
as the glasses were filled and left to dribble around
unmopped, or the glasses of wine which took thirty-five
minutes to turn up. Perhaps, at the bar, time moves more
slowly than in the restaurant.

Halfway through our main course we were asked if
we wanted more bread. We pointed out we hadn't had
the first lot yet, and so it was finally offered, complete

61

with a hunk of butter in a water-slicked dish. We ordered a side of dauphinoise potatoes and were brought instead some slippery, creamed spinach because, apparently, the dauphinoise was finished. The waiter returned. Actually it wasn't finished. They just forgot to put through the order and so here it is now: hunks of undercooked potato in a bath of salty cream with a lid of waxy cheese.

A couple of the dishes on the menu are marked by a chemistry-set icon, to indicate that these are chef Julian Ward's 'British classics with a twist' – the twist being that they were very nasty indeed. I punctured a poached egg, presented with a coating of Welsh rarebit, and out poured transparent raw egg white. Not cooking an egg. Now that really is a neat twist for a restaurant. The twist in 'Julian's Vegetable Lasagne' was that it didn't contain pasta. Instead it was a dense block of finely mandolined root vegetables that tasted mostly of salt and pepper and effortless regret.

Other dishes had twists too, whether advertised or not. The twist in the lobster fish cakes was the impossibility of finding evidence of the lobster without recourse to the sort of sensitive equipment they doubtless keep locked away in the basement. The fish cakes were hockey-puck sized, shaped and, in a deft act of consistency, textured. They were dry and dense. I could have hurt a member of staff if I'd lobbed one. I considered it. The twist in the monkfish dish was that the crust of black olive and mustard seed completely obliterated any flavour the heavily overcooked fish might have had.

The one stray molecule of good taste in the kitchen lay at the dessert stage. Granted, they were all nursery-food-style soft things in pots but they were nice soft things: a good rice pudding, a soft, warm chocolate mousse and a good crème brûlée, sadly ruined by being flavoured with an almost artificial-tasting extract of pistachio.

Any enjoyment to be taken from these dishes was completely undermined, however, by the arrival at our table of the chef, who told us the manager had said he should come over to ask us how lunch was. OK, so they had recognized me. But given I'd been sending back half-eaten plates of food and responding honestly, when asked why, that I didn't think it was very nice, what was ever going to be gained? How was that exchange ever going to end well? Like so much else here, it was a really stupid idea. Unwilling to be drawn, I was reduced to telling him that I had indeed eaten lunch. With you lot, however, I can be a little more candid. Let's just say I ate that lunch so you wouldn't have to.

The Royal Institution eventually came to their senses and abandoned the Time and Space concept. They replaced it with a rather sensible-looking restaurant/café serving an all-day menu.

March 2007

Langtry's, 21 Pont Street, London SW1. Telephone: 020 7201 6619. Meal for two, including wine and service, £80.

There was a funereal air to the deserted entrance hall at Langtry's. When I received my starter I understood why.

The whole place was in mourning for the wasted lives of the Morecambe Bay brown shrimps that had been sacrificed to make it. Langtry's, part of the Cadogan Hotel, occupies what was once the Knightsbridge home of Lillie Langtry, actress and famed squeeze of Queen Victoria's eldest boy, and uses that as the cue for a menu of British dishes, among them the prawn cocktail. I hadn't had a good one in ages and I'm afraid I still haven't. For this was not any old prawn cocktail. This was 'Langtry's prawn cocktail', the 'signature dish' of their head chef Robert Lyon who, the website tells us, has a passion for creating 'interesting and innovative dishes'. Oh how I wish that he didn't.

What arrived was a highball glass, piled with hot battered prawns, their delicate flavour mislaid in the deep-fat fryer. Underneath that was a cloyingly sweet Marie Rose sauce ice cream – there are good reasons for not making ice cream out of mayonnaise and tomato ketchup, not least politeness – then a layer of avocado cream, and finally, a plug of underpowered shellfish jelly. From this I can tell you that Langtry's does indeed celebrate British food, but only in the way a murderer might dance upon its victim's grave.

I recognize the pressures that lie upon the shoulders of young chefs employed to make a splash in London's fraught restaurant market. They read about Heston Blumenthal's deconstructions and re-engineerings at the Fat Duck, and they think, 'I can do this too.' When the truth is, few of them can. I beg any young chef to ask themselves two questions before reinterpreting a classic dish: is their version an improvement on what went before?

And does it, at the very least, make us look at the traditional version anew? If the answer to either of these is no, and with this prawn cocktail it is 'no' in pink neon letters ten feet high, then Please Don't Do It. (I'm also minded to ban chefs under a certain age from eating at the Fat Duck in case they get ideas they lack the skills to execute.)

The problem at Langtry's is not just lousy concepts, but inconsistency. A starter of beef tea – though we can call it beef consommé, what with it not being 1893 out there no more, guv – had a lovely intense depth of flavour. There was, however, nothing lovely about their toad in the hole. Instead of sausages there was a fillet of pork crusted, for reasons which escape me, in almonds. All it made me think was how nice toad in the hole is, and how nice this wasn't. The Yorkshire pudding was burnt around the edges, and dumped inside was Savoy cabbage with shards of bacon. Like the Yorkshire, a stuffed pheasant leg in my main course was overdone, though slices of the breast and some creamed kale showed they can get other things right. At the end, the filling in a custard tart was pleasingly heavy on the nutmeg – though, proving themselves reliably unreliable, the pastry was stiff and heavy – and a rhubarb ripple ice cream lacked any tooth-sucking tartness. It costs £21 for three courses, which is only good value if you lost your taste buds to a threshing machine.

All in all, a gloomy meal in a gloomy spot. They have retained the original plaster features but painted them battleship grey, and surrounded them with the sort of fake Rocco chairs, upholstered in primary colours, that

Victoria Beckham might think are classy and I don't. The surprisingly cheerful staff, given the lack of custom, are of the sort who think asking you how everything is when you are in the middle of a conversation is the same as good service. I have been criticized in the past for picking on staff who are, I am told, only doing their job. Nevertheless I will make one observation. Letting a waiter out into the room with grim, lank, greasy hair slicked to his head suggests that nobody in management really cares. It is not an aid to the digestion. Then again, at this restaurant, not much is.

The Cadogan Hotel eventually closed Langtry's and reopened the restaurant as a showcase for ingredients that had been recognized in the Great Taste Awards. A panel of food journalists, restaurant critics and commentators was invited to be part of a supervising panel, overseeing the selection of those ingredients. I was not among them. It too has since closed.

June 2000

Spoon at Sanderson, 50 Berners Street, London W1. Telephone: 020 7300 1400. Price of dinner for two, including wine and service, whatever the management thinks it can get away with.

Whenever a critic writes a review of a restaurant in one of the achingly hip hotels owned by Ian Schrager – the man behind the Royalton in New York, St Martin's Lane in London and now the Sanderson on a site just north of Oxford Street – a handwritten card arrives, as if from the man himself. The one I received after I expressed my complete disdain for Asia de Cuba at St Martin's Lane said something like: 'Please do try us again,' which was, and remains, a victory of hope over expectation.

Can I suggest, Mr Schrager, that when you come to sending me a card after this review of Spoon at Sanderson it says: 'I apologize for running such a nasty money-grabbing operation.' For Spoon is, without doubt, the most outrageous exercise in separating punters from their cash currently at work in the capital. Not that the punters appear to mind; it took me three weeks to get a table. Spoon is what they call hot.

The night I went there, the bar, a grand rectangular affair of onyx and shimmering lights, was packed with the sort of people who prefer mirrors on the horizontal rather than the vertical, the better to powder their noses. Perhaps they are also the kind of people who don't notice prices, for it is here that the outrages begin. While I waited for my companion I ordered a glass of South African Sauvignon Blanc. I was told it was £7.50 and, swallowing hard, handed over a tenner. I got back £1.40. I looked at the receipt. Apparently a 15 per cent discretionary service charge had been added to my bill. For the serving of a glass of wine at the bar. This is one way to guarantee that a fine glass of white wine will leave a nasty taste in the mouth.

Thus fleeced, we were led to the dining room, which, again, is a clever space of pale shades in which everybody can look at everybody else. The menus, like the prices, are of staggering proportions. If you were caught in a forest on a rainy night one of these could easily serve as a bivouac. But then the menu needs to be big to contain the silliness within. I had always thought that one of the reasons for going to a restaurant is so that clever people, who know how to cook, can come up with lots of interesting ways to combine interesting ingredients. Not at Spoon.

The great Alain Ducasse, who has sired not one but two restaurants in France, each boasting three Michelin stars, is here the consultant. His big idea is to break dishes up into their ingredients and then let you mix and match. Or, as the illiterate menu puts it, 'If you are like switching and changing we invite you to zig zag through the different columns and think the unthinkable.'

For our starters we were not yet brave enough to really go for it so we chose two of the non-fragmented dishes. I had pork and shrimp ravioli with a piquant tomato sauce, which were fine, the kind of thing you could find in Chinatown for £3.50, and certainly not fine enough for a price tag of £14. My companion's ceviche of sea bass – the fish 'cooked' in a citrus marinade – was rather good: delicate, fresh, succulent. As it should be for £16.

For my main course I decided to try and think the unthinkable by combining the grilled saddle of lamb at £20 with the truffle sauce that was meant to go with the veal, and the macaroni cheese which, after tasting it, I concluded should not have gone with anything. I was intrigued to see how the kitchen would bring this ad-libbed set of ingredients together. The answer is they don't. The lamb and the solid gummy strip of macaroni cheese were situated half a foot away from each other on the plate like a dysfunctional married couple on the verge of divorce. As to the sauce, that came in a little bowl on the side, complete with a congealed skin, which was attractive. My companion's grilled squid (a mere £17) came with the same tomato sauce as with my starter and a little splodge of truly nasty mango gunk.

The wine list has nothing below £20. We chose the second cheapest, a bottle of New Zealand Sauvignon Blanc at £23. Spoon clearly didn't think this was enough. It appeared on the bill as £45, bringing the total including that 'discretionary' service charge to around £165. I complained. The bill went down to £136. I gave them my credit card. Back came the receipt with the service-charge box left open. I knocked the tip down to 10 per cent. When they saw what I had done all hell let loose. What had happened, they asked? What had they done? I explained. Oh, they said. After a five-minute pause they announced they would denote my table 'non-service'. Hence a bill of £119.

Many of you could be forgiven for becoming rather tired of the recent run of reviews: new London restaurants, each worse than the last, throwing up bills well north of £100. For what it's worth I see this and the previous two as a kind of trilogy, a description of what happens when the economics of restaurants becomes so perverse that the last thing to matter is the food. It's tiresome and it's depressing and I too have had enough of it. Normal service will now resume. Promise.

Ian Schrager did write to me again, but it was not to apologize. It was to complain that, by revealing the contents of the previous letter, I had betrayed a confidence. Spoon eventually closed to be replaced at the Sanderson by a Malaysian-inspired restaurant called Suka. I didn't like it much either. After that review Mr Schrager did not bother to write. Suka has also since been replaced.

February 2012

Novikov London, 50a Berkeley Street, London W1. Telephone: 020 7399 4330. Meal for two, including wine and service, £160.

You could, if you wished, hate Novikov London on principle. Arkady Novikov, whose name is above the door, owns fifty or so restaurants in Moscow and likes to boast of his connections to Vladimir Putin. He has talked to me of his work as outside caterer to Putin's Kremlin and a few years ago had to break off from an interview with me to entertain Putin's wife, Lyudmila, to a tour of his next venue. She showed an almost proprietorial interest in the curtains and the silverware. Of course, Putin has been accused in diplomatic cables released by WikiLeaks of turning Russia into a wretched kleptocracy. He persecuted violent campaigns in Chechnya full of vile human rights abuses and is currently being fingered for nicking Russia's parliamentary elections. If we know a man by the company he keeps, then perhaps the arrival in London of a big-ticket Novikov restaurant is not something to be universally applauded.

But you really don't have to hate Novikov on principle. There's more than enough about the place to let you hate it on its own terms. There is the usual stupidity of booking a table for 9 p.m. only to be told that your booking is for just two hours. There is the unusual stupidity of approaching the steps and an ape in a bomber jacket with an earpiece shoving his body between you and the door and barking: 'Are you eating here tonight?' To which I could but reply: 'Only if you'll let me.' We get inside and more people step in our way. But we are spotted and led through the crowds. Novikov is vast. Indeed it is two restaurants in one. The front half is a pan-Asian place that serves a menu of Chinese, Malaysian and Japanese dishes as if they are all the same thing (including the highly endangered bluefin tuna. Don't look so surprised. Novikov feeds Putin. You think he'd care about a small thing like sustainability?).

Down a flight of stairs, past the crowds of young ladies with older gentlemen sucking the bar dry, and you are in the huge windowless Italian restaurant, denoted by bits of wrought-iron, hanging faux-rustic chandeliers, a huge open kitchen with meat-hanging cabinets, and the bash and clatter of music so loud I feel it in my prostate gland. It reminds me of the mega restaurants of Las Vegas, with one crucial difference. In Vegas the restaurants are generally very good. There's too much competition for it to be otherwise. This is generally very, very bad: prices that knock the wind out of you and moments of cooking so cack-handed, so foul, so astoundingly grim, you want to congratulate the kitchen on their incompetence.

We eat some good things. Their version of vitello tonnato – thinly sliced veal with an anchovy and tuna sauce – gets the approval of my companion, who has a house in Italy. Fried mushrooms topped with duck eggs is fine too, as it should be for £18.50. It isn't in any way Italian. More towards Gascony. If only they'd stayed there. We order both a rabbit ragout with pappardelle and calf's liver with butter and sage. We taste both platefuls. My companion looks at me and says: 'This tastes like cheap Chinese food.' She's right.

It takes me a minute to nail the rabbit dish: the small gnarly bits of meat, the thick, heavy sauce that tastes as if it has been thickened with cornflower, the weird hit of chicken flavour I usually associate with stock cubes. It's a chicken and mushroom pot noodle. Without the useful plastic pot. The liver dish has all the same vices. The tragedy is that, underneath the wallpaper-paste sauce is some very good liver that has ended its life badly. Zucchini fritti are so much hot, wet, floppy saltiness. We finish with a pile of formless Italian meringue. The hit of sugar feels like a reward. The wine list is punishing, and includes bottles which retail in Italy for €8, priced here at £50. Waiters are impeccably Italian in that they will argue with you. Dishes are mispriced between the menu and the bill.

And the most depressing thing? It's full; packed to the fake ironwork with the hooting and the stamping, the depilated, the bronzed and Botoxed. And so my advice to you. Don't go to Novikov. Keep not going. Keep not going a lot. In a city with a talent for opening hateful and tasteless restaurants, Novikov marks a special new low. That's its real achievement.

For what it's worth A. A. Gill of the Sunday Times *liked Novikov London very much. He gave it four out of five stars.*